# WINNER'S PLAYBOOK

(A COLLECTION OF ESSAYS ON VICTORY)

ESSAY TWO

# ILLUMINATION

BY

MICHAEL NORDMAN

ESSAY TWO

# ILLUMINATION

ISBN: 979-8-9959169-1-8



UNITED STATES

## Forward

There are books that merely provide information, and then there are books that invite the reader into reflection, prayer, and deeper spiritual awareness. *Illumination* by Michael Nordman belongs in the second category.

Throughout these pages, Michael repeatedly directs the reader back to the central truth that Christianity is not simply about external religion, intellectual achievement, or human effort. Rather, it is about the living presence of Christ working within His people through the Holy Spirit and through the Word of God. Again and again, the reader is encouraged not only to read Scripture, but to approach it prayerfully, expectantly, and with a heart open to God's transforming work.

One of the strengths of this essay is its passion. Michael writes with conviction that faith is not dead tradition, but a living relationship with the risen Christ. He reminds believers that God still teaches, guides, strengthens, and comforts His people through His Spirit. In a distracted and noisy world, this call to slow down, meditate on Scripture, and seek the illumination of God is both timely and needed.

Readers will notice the broad Christian voices woven throughout the work — references ranging from the Apostles, to Martin Luther, to Lectio Divina, to historic confessions of faith. Though traditions may differ in language and emphasis, the common thread remains the same: believers throughout history have recognized their dependence upon God to open the eyes of the heart and reveal the riches of His grace.

At its core, this book is an invitation. An invitation to seek Christ more deeply. An invitation to approach Scripture with humility and expectation. And ultimately, an invitation to discover that the Christian life is not sustained merely by human striving, but by the grace, love, and power of God Himself.

Whether you agree with every conclusion presented or not, my encouragement is this: read thoughtfully, search the Scriptures, pray earnestly, and allow this work to challenge you to draw nearer to Christ.

May the Lord grant every reader wisdom, discernment, and a deeper awareness of His presence.

Rev. Nathan Lewis
CEO, Tselem Ministries
The Hiding Place Retreat Center
Sturgeon Bay, Wisconsin

# CHOSEN

A few chosen ones will realize
that it is God's will for the saints to be likeminded and speak
the same thing, the TRUTH.
The bold, the few, those who love God, those who are called
according to God's purpose, those with a spiritual resolve
and fearless courage due to love, the faithful will see this
need to embrace
the Word of God illuminated by the Holy Spirit
as a means or the path to the unity of the saints.

"Many are called but few are chosen"
Jesus

CHOSEN MEANS YOU ARE SELECTED

What does this even mean?

**Blessed be the God and Father of our Lord
Jesus Christ, who hath blessed us with all
spiritual blessings in heavenly places in Christ:
4 According as he hath chosen us in him before
the foundation of the world, that we should be
holy and without blame before him in love:
5 Having predestinated us unto the adoption of
children by Jesus Christ to himself, according
to the good pleasure of his will,
6 To the praise of the glory of his grace,
wherein he hath made us accepted (highly
favored) in the beloved.**

**Ephesians 1:3-6 KJV**

## HOW DO YOU MAKE SELECTION?
### (HOW DO YOU GET CHOSEN?)

To be holy and blameless before him...

**HOW** can anyone? All have sinned and come short of the glory of God. How can anyone? How can anyone be holy and blameless? If being holy by your own volition was a requirement for salvation (selection), then there wouldn't even be 144 thousand saved, no one could be saved except **JESUS!**

It definitely is NOT

by one's own righteousness!

Romans 10:3 KJV, For they being ignorant of God's righteousness, and going about to establish their own righteousness, have not submitted themselves unto the righteousness of God.

This means that to **QUALIFY FOR SELECTION** holiness and blamelessness are <u>not</u> something **YOU** bring to the table when you are summoned (called) by

the LORD to the selection process, which was decided and planned out by God, in His foreknowledge before the creation of the universe.

So, **HOW** do you get selected?

# WHAT DO WE DO?

By grace, through faith...

## RECEIVE THE GIFT

FAITH COMES OUT OF THE REPORT, THE REPORT THROUGH THE WORD OF CHRIST.

(Ref. Romans 10:17)

KEY POINT TO NOTE;

JESUS PAID FOR THE SINS OF THE WHOLE WORLD.

(REF. 1 JOHN 2:1-2)

SINCE JESUS IS YOUR ADVOCATE, HE NOMINATED YOU AND SUPPORTS YOUR ACCEPTANCE TO THE SPIRITUAL SPECIAL FORCES PROGRAM.

FINE PRINT;

IN ORDER TO PASS "SELECTION" YOU HAVE TO REALIZE THAT YOU ARE NOT QUALIFIED TO RECEIVE THE GIFT WHICH QUALIFIES YOU, WHICH IS THE MYSTERY-CHRIST IN YOU. IT IS THE LOVE AND KINDNESS OF GOD WHICH ATTRACTS YOU AND LEADS YOU AWAY FROM OR TURNS YOU, LIKE AN INFORMANT FOR THE FBI OR AN ASSET FOR MILITARY REGEIM CHANGE. YOU TURN FROM THE CARNAL MINDSET OF THE WORLD AND GET TRANSLATED INTO THE KINGDOM OF LIGHT. YOU SWITCH SIDES BECAUSE GOD'S KINDNESS GIVES YOU HOPE, THE ONLY HOPE AVAILABLE TO THE HUMAN RACE.

If you are a chosen one (selected), you will have "the faith" … the faith of Jesus Christ. ① When you have Christ in you, you become "one" with him. His Spirit is so intertwined with your spirit that his faith becomes your faith. This happens in the invisible supernatural dimensions of reality IN YOUR SPIRIT. ②

① Galatians 2:20b, And the life which I now live in the flesh I live by the faith of the Son of God, who loved me, and gave himself for me.

② Now may the God of peace himself sanctify you completely, and may your whole spirit and soul and body be kept blameless at the coming of our Lord Jesus Christ. [24] He who calls you is faithful; he will surely do it. 1 Thes. 5:23-24.

Then, when you read, for example, Romans 3: 21-22 (KJV) you see what I'm talking about.

But now the righteousness of God
without the law is manifested,
being witnessed by the law and the prophets;
22 Even the righteousness of God
which is by faith of Jesus Christ
unto all and upon all them that believe:
for there is no difference:

This Verse in Galatians 2:20 (KJV) makes more sense now too, in light of the Mystery,

I am crucified with Christ:
nevertheless I live; yet not I,
but Christ liveth in me:
and the life which I now live in the flesh
I live by the faith of the Son of God③,
who loved me, and gave himself for me.

---

③ This is why the Mystery is called the Mystery of the Faith (1 Timothy 3:9) Look it up! This is a requirement of any elder, deacon, or any leader.

## CHECK THIS OUT!

Knowing that a man is not justified
by the works of the law,
but by the faith of Jesus Christ,
even we have believed in Jesus Christ,
that we might be justified by the faith of Christ,
and not by the works of the law:
for by the works of the law
shall no flesh be justified.

Galatians 2:16 KJV

**AS YOU CAN SEE,
THERE IS A
SUPERNATURAL
THING GOING ON HERE.**

THIS IS **HOW** YOU
MAKE SELECTION
OR GET CHOSEN,
BY RECEIVING
THE GIFT OF CHRIST IN YOU,
THE PROMISED HOLY SPIRIT.

This is how the promise can be sure to all the seed.

That the blessing of Abraham
might come on the Gentiles
through Jesus Christ
that we might receive
the promise of the Spirit
through faith.

Galatians 3:14 KJV

Jesus gave us a parable to think about concerning this. It will take some deep thought to understand what he was talking about, but you can get it.

## THE PARABLE OF THE WEDDING FEAST

And again Jesus spoke to them in parables, saying, 2 "The
kingdom of heaven may be compared to a king who gave a
wedding feast for his son, 3 and sent his servants to call
those who were invited to the wedding feast, but they
would not come. 4 Again he sent other servants, saying, 'Tell
those who are invited, "See, I have prepared my dinner, my
oxen and my fat calves have been slaughtered, and
everything is ready. Come to the wedding feast."' 5 But they
paid no attention and went off, one to his farm, another to
his business, 6 while the rest seized his servants, treated
them shamefully, and killed them. 7 The king was angry, and
he sent his troops and destroyed those murderers and
burned their city. 8 Then he said to his servants, 'The
wedding feast is ready, but those invited were not worthy.
9 Go therefore to the main roads and invite to the wedding
feast as many as you find.' 10 And those servants went out
into the roads and gathered all whom they found, both bad
and good. So the wedding hall was filled with guests.
11 "But when the king came in to look at the guests, he saw
there a man who had no wedding garment. 12 And he said to
him, 'Friend, how did you get in here without a wedding
garment?' And he was speechless. 13 Then the king said to

the attendants, 'Bind him hand and foot and cast him into the outer darkness. In that place there will be weeping and gnashing of teeth.' [14] **For many are called, but few are chosen."**

Matthew 22:1-14 ESV

Here we see that those who responded positively to the invitation by going to the wedding feast were the chosen ones and how important it is to be clothed with the right garments. Don't want to be "that guy" without the right wedding garments.

**DOES THIS MEAN**
**THAT WE ARE TO PUT ON CHRIST?**

THIS SHOWS US HOW

ABSOLUTELY IMPORTANT IT IS

TO READ THE BIBLE

AND GET A TRUE UNDERSTANDING OF WHAT

IT MEANS,

BY THE HOLY SPIRIT,

THE WAY GOD INTENDED

US TO READ THE BIBLE.

BE CLOTHED WITH HIM.
JESUS IS THE GARMENT YOU NEED[4]

...AS MANY AS HAVE BEEN BAPTIZED INTO CHRIST
HAVE PUT ON CHRIST.

---

④ I will greatly rejoice in the LORD, my soul shall be joyful in my God; for he hath clothed me with the garments of salvation, he hath covered me with the robe of righteousness, as a bridegroom decketh himself with ornaments, and as a bride adorneth herself with her jewels. Isaiah 61:10 KJV. The Old Testament is fulfilled in the Mystery-Christ in you.

## LOVE is our main power to win.

When you have Christ in you you have the ability to access supernatural love, the love of God in Christ Jesus, and get energized by His Spirit so you have victory in every situation.

That he would grant you,
according to the riches of his glory,
to be strengthened with might
by his Spirit in the inner man;
17 That Christ may dwell in your hearts by faith; that
ye, being rooted and grounded in love,
18 May be able to comprehend with all saints what is
the breadth, and length, and depth, and height;
19 And to know **the love of Christ**,
which passeth knowledge (it is supernatural),
that ye might be filled with
all the fulness of God.

Ephesians 3:16-19 KJV

# LOVE NEVER FAILS

Everyone does not have this superpower. It is available to everyone but only those who are disciples of Jesus Christ have this superpower (of divine love), those who are clothed with Christ. It is given to you by God through the Spirit when Christ lives in your heart. **REAL TALK** This is one way you know you are chosen[5]; you have this love which passes knowledge. This is the power of the Glad Tidings or the Gospel; the UNSEARCHABLE RICHES OF CHRIST. This is what the Bible is about. Not a behavior modification program. It is a life-giving eternal spiritual adventure with Jesus Christ. You get this through the Glad Tidings, the words in/of Holy Scripture, the Good Public Announcement about God's love, kindness, and grace for you through Jesus Christ.

The energizing of this supernatural power is given as a gift by the grace of God to all the saints. (Do you have it yet?)

---

[5] Beloved, let us love one another: for love is of God; and every one that loveth is born of God, and knoweth God. 1 John 4:7 KJV

The **POWER** of God is accessed through the WORD OF GOD. His power is unlocked for us when we pray and ask for it while we are reading or hearing God's Word.

# THIS IS THE KEY TO VICTORY

Thou therefore, my son, bc strong
in the grace that is in Christ Jesus.
2 And the things that thou hast heard of me
among many witnesses, the same commit thou
to faithful men,
who shall be able to teach others also.
3 Thou therefore endure hardness,
as a good soldier of Jesus Christ.
4 No man that warreth

entangleth himself with the affairs of this life;
that he may please him
who hath chosen him to be a soldier.
5 And if a man also strive for masteries,
yet is he not crowned, except he strive lawfully.
6 The husbandman that laboureth
must be first partaker of the fruits.
7 Consider what I say;
And
**the Lord give thee understanding
in all things.**

2 Timothy 2:1-7 KJV

Every valuable tradition of Christianity at one time or another practiced this method of attracting the phenomenon of God's interaction through prayer and meditation, reflection, or pondering Scripture.

In much of the world today it is a lost art.

If you want to have **VICTORY** in the supernatural battlefield (and the Gospel is a supernatural Gospel not just a bunch of dead words) you will want to embrace this wonderful blessing of God's grace.

## God's Word is alive!

When we prayerfully approach our reading of Scripture, asking God to open the eyes of our hearts[6] to understand what the Scriptures mean, like Jesus did back in the day with his disciples[7], God will engage with you and help you.

The thing which all Christians have in common is Christ in you-the Mystery. The Holy Spirit, the Word of God, and love are the only things which will unite or are actually uniting believers (saints).

⑥ Having the eyes of your hearts enlightened. Ephesians 1:18 ESV

⑦ Then he opened their minds to understand the Scriptures. Luke 24:45 ESV

The Catholic Christians call it LECTIO DIVINA which is Latin for DIVINE READING. This is practiced today by many Catholics.

## How to Pray with Lectio Divina

"It's important to remember that *Lectio Divina* is not a Bible Study, where you research and interpret the Bible from a theological or historical perspective. Rather, *Lectio Divina* is a personal conversation with God through scripture... Ask the Holy Spirit to help guide you through this experience!"

Martin Luther wrote in a letter to his friend once quoting Jesus who was quoting the Prophets saying, “And they shall be all taught of God”.

Here’s the full quote.
“We cannot attain to the understanding of Scripture either by study or strength of intellect. Therefore your first duty must be to begin with prayer. Entreat the Lord to deign to grant you, in his rich mercy, rightly to understand his word. There is no other interpreter of the word but the Author of that word himself. Even as he has said, ‘**They shall be all taught of God.**’ Hope nothing from your study and strength of intellect; but simply put your trust in God, and in the guidance of his Spirit.”

The Orthodox Catholic Christians call it ILLUMINATION.

ST DIADOCHOS OF PHOTIKI put it like this,
"Spiritual discourse fully satisfies our intellectual perception, because it comes from God through the energy of love. It is on account of this that the intellect continues undisturbed in its concentration on theology. It does not suffer then from the emptiness which produces a state of anxiety, since in its contemplation it is filled to the degree that the energy of love desires. So it is right always to wait, with a faith energized by love, for the illumination which will enable us to speak. **For nothing is so destitute as a mind philosophizing about God when it is without Him."**

The Westminster Confession of Faith puts it like this, "Nevertheless we acknowledge the inward **illumination of the Spirit of God** to be necessary for the saving understanding of such things as are revealed in the Word."

Westminster Assembly 1644

## *Who else should we include?*

The Apostle John did it, the Apostle Paul and the saints did it, Jesus did it, even King David did it.

This is a critical practice which we must employ to be winners in the faith. Like a Navy Seal being able to swim.

In a special place in your soul, where your spirit touches your soul, God interacts with you through His Word and His Holy Spirit when you pray and ask Him to.

I love you.

When you see things happen in real time happen as a result of your prayers and time in Scripture, you will know that/when it is God doing things.

Here are some ways the Holy Spirit INTERACTS.

- He brings things to your remembrance.
- An urging (like to go to a certain Scripture).
- It clicks with other things He is showing you.
- A revelation [(a picture, words, a knowing) often times in an unsolicited unexpected manner].
- He illuminates the words with love so everything comes alive and things are imparted to you.
- He kindles faith, zeal, transformation, joy… love (a comforting joy that He is teaching you).
- The Holy Spirit simply gives you an understanding. Often times something which was hidden in plain sight, so simple, so obvious, you wonder why you didn't see that before.
- Other ways.

How is He working in you? Write that down and pray for more of that, so you can grow in your relationship with Him.

That He may give YOU,

According to the riches of His

glory,

With POWER to be

strengthened

by His SPIRIT in the inner

man

To reside THE CHRIST,

through faith,

In your hearts, in love being

(you are) rooted and founded

that YOU may be

Fully able to apprehend

With all the saints... what is
the breadth and length and
height and depth,
And know the surpassing
knowledge
LOVE OF CHRIST;
THAT YOU MAY BE
FILLED
WITH ALL THE
FULNESS OF GOD.
Ephesians

ZAP!
WOW
YOU KNOW HOW READING
ENGAGES YOUR IMAGINATION?
READING SCRIPTURE
ENGAGES YOUR IMAGINATION
WITH THE SPIRIT OF GOD.
boom

## You can get started any time you want.

Here is a prayer you can say;

Abba Father,

I pray that I get it.
I ask that You
open the eyes of my heart
so, I can see...
that the revelation of the Mystery
of Christ in Me,
and the Gospel of Grace,
be illuminated in me,
that You give me understanding
of Your will
and engage with me as I read
and meditate on Your Holy Scripture,
written to me.

In the Name of Jesus, Amen.

The Holy Spirit unlocks the Faith of Christ in Holy Scriptures into your heart, and the Life of Christ is manifested in your soul. This is how we are transformed. This is how we engage our spirit through prayer while reading Scripture. All the benefits, blessings, favor, power, prayers, and standards written in the books of the Bible written to you are yours.

**Jesus foretold that it would be for you.**

But the Helper, the Holy Spirit,
whom the Father will send in my name, he
will teach you all things
and bring to your remembrance
all that I have said to you.
John 14:26

Read what Jesus said about the Holy Spirit.

And I say unto you, Ask, and it shall be given you;
seek, and ye shall find; knock,
and it shall be opened unto you.
10 For every one that asks receives; and he that seeks
finds; and to him that knocks
it shall be opened.
11 If a son shall ask bread of any of you that is a
father, will he give him a stone? or if *he ask* a fish,
will he for a fish give him a serpent?
12 Or if he shall ask an egg,
will he offer him a scorpion?

[13] If ye then, being evil, know how to give good gifts unto your children, how much more shall *your* heavenly Father give the Holy Spirit to those that ask him?

Luke 11:9-13 KJV

And we know that the Son of God has come and has given us understanding, so that we may know him who is true; and we are in him who is true, in his Son Jesus Christ. He is the true God and eternal life. [21] Little children, keep yourselves from idols.

1 John 5:20 ESV

LOOK FOR FUTURE ESSAYS

ON

VICTORY

UNITEDSAINTSOFAMERICA.CHURCH,

WEAREUNDERGRACE.COM,

OR

AMAZON

**AND TELL YOUR FRIENDS ABOUT THIS.**

BIBLIOGRAPHY

**Special thanks to the Holy Spirit of the Living God who inspired this essay and opens the eyes of our heart.**

**The ESV**® Bible (The Holy Bible, English Standard Version®), © 2001 by Crossway, ESV Text Edition: 2025.
**Interlinear Bible** from Bible Hub @ biblehub.com.
**Public Domain**: King James Version **(KJV),** Darby Translation **(DARBY).**
**How to pray with Lectio Divina**
https://www.dynamiccatholic.com/about-lectio-divina.html
**The Westminster Confession of Faith**
Thewestminsterstandard.org
( I.Of the Holy Scripture, VI The whole counsel of God...)
**St Diadochos of Photiki** quote from The Philokalia Volume One, page 254, Faber and Faber, ISBN 0-71-11377-x. © The Eling Trust 1979
**Martin Luther Quote**
The Spirit of Prophecy, by Ellen G White, vol. 4, p. 68 [*108*]
© Ellen G White Estate

**ART CREDITS**

**SHUTTERSTOCK**

Flag by Militarist.

Flaming Sword (modified) by Macrovector.

Camo for Cover (modified) by Shutterstock AI.

A Happy black lady received package, unpacking cardboard by Lopolo.

Teamwork, collaboration and uniting efforts concept BY Alphavector.

Thoughtful young Asian woman with Bible in living room by Pixel-Shot.

AMEN speech bubble (modified) by Barrirret.

Bronze Relief of Luther translating the Bible. Lutherdenkmal statue in Eisleben, his birth and death place, Germany. Monument by Rudolf Siemering (1883). Pic by Anastazzo.

**VECTOR STOCK**

Comic Girl Portrait Vector Image by Stonepic Retro.

Surprised Doctor Comic Portrait Vector Image (modified) by Rogistok.

Flaming Sword (modified) by Macrovector

Westminster Abby by Imagepluss

**MAGNIFIC**

Young-woman-reading-book-library by Magnific AI.

**ARMY PHOTO**

221107-F-PO220-1007.JPG Photo By: Staff Sgt. Noshoba Davi

This photograph is considered public domain and has been cleared for release.

**DREAMSTIME**

Cheerful-ai-generated-emoji-icon-big-smile-two-thumbs-up-expressing-happiness-approval-emoji-icon-thumbs-up-imageRamu Chinnasamy

Smiling-woman-open-lock-huge-key-young-happy-businesswoman-use-tool-padlock-opening-problem-solution-vector-illustration by Drawlab19

Bold-comic-style-exclamation-mark-illustration-dynamic-vibrant-expressive-lines-colors by Oleksii Bezrodnii

Stock-photo-monk-prayer-benedictine-reading-bible-monastic-church-great-evening-light-peaceful-atmosphere-image © Nicolas Bancillon.
Woman-sitting-steps-reading-book-young-adult-arab-ethnic-alone-human-scarf-veil-sacred-old-life-hope-light-seat by Maryna Kriuchenko.
Stock-photo-navy-seals-insignia-trident-coveted-badge-u-s-resting-american-flag-patch-united-states-patch by Rebelq.
Pop-art-background-place-text-comic-book-frame-cartoon-retro-vector-illustration-drawing-advertising-image © Timea Adel Bajko.
Stock-images-girl-reading-bible-image © Justin Skinner.
**Photo of Young Boy Reading the Bible** by Victoria Robel.
**FRONT COVER** by Michael Nordman

# FOR CHRIST'S SAKE

www.ingramcontent.com/pod-product-compliance
Lightning Source LLC
LaVergne TN
LVHW052310100826
845147LV00006B/725

* 9 7 9 8 9 9 5 9 1 6 9 1 8 *